step-by-step
chicken

p

This is a Parragon Book
First published in 2002

Parragon
Queen Street House
4 Queen Street
Bath BA1 1HE, UK

ISBN: 0-75255-004-3

Printed in Spain

Produced by The Bridgewater Book Company Ltd, Lewes, East Sussex

Acknowledgements
Creative Director Terry Jeavons
Art Director Sarah Howerd
Editorial Director Fiona Biggs
Senior Editor Mark Truman
Editorial Assistants Simon Bailey, Tom Kitch
Page Make-up Chris Akroyd

NOTES FOR THE READER

- This book uses both metric and imperial measurements. Follow the same units of measurement throughout; do not mix metric and imperial.
- All spoon measurements are level: teaspoons are assumed to be 5 ml, and table-spoons are assumed to be 15 ml.
- Unless otherwise stated, milk is assumed to be full-fat, eggs and individual vegetables such as potatoes are medium-sized, and pepper is freshly ground black pepper.
- Recipes using raw or very lightly cooked eggs should be avoided by infants, the elderly, pregnant women, convalescents, and anyone suffering from an illness.
- Optional ingredients, variations, and serving suggestions have not been included in the calculations.
- The times given are an approximate guide only. Preparation times differ according to the techniques used by different people and the cooking times vary as a result of the type of oven used.

Contents

Introduction

When it comes to planning meals that are quick and easy to prepare and cook, chicken can be a star ingredient. A chicken portion may be prepared very simply in numerous ways: brushed with olive oil and grilled, and served with rice and a side salad, or roasted in the oven with herbs and served with potatoes and vegetables. A chicken breast makes the ultimate easy meal. It may be cut into strips and and added to a stir-fry, or added to pasta or risotto. Chicken Risotto à la Milanese is made with saffron, producing a lovely golden colour.

If you want to prepare your meal and pop it in the oven while you have a long soak in the bath after a busy day, use chicken as a base for a hearty soup, such as Wild Rice & Smoked Chicken Chowder, or for a casserole such as Chicken Basquaise, in which chicken and rice are cooked together in one pot.

guide to recipe key	
easy	Recipes are graded as follows: 1 pea = easy; 2 peas = very easy; 3 peas = extremely easy.
serves 4	Recipes generally serve four people. Simply halve the ingredients to serve two, taking care not to mix imperial and metric measurements.
15 minutes	Preparation time. Where recipes include marinating, soaking, standing, or chilling, times for these are listed separately: eg., 15 minutes, plus 1 hour to marinate.
15 minutes	Cooking time. Cooking times do not include the cooking of rice served with the main dishes.

For an informal meal for guests, recipes like Murgh Pullau or Jambalaya are fun, and for an elegant dinner try Poussins with Fruity Rice Stuffing. This dish traditionally uses game hens from Cornwall in southwest England, stuffed with rice and chestnuts, raisins and apricots, and flavoured with port.

Chicken is inexpensive, low in fat, and easy to digest, so it fits perfectly into a busy modern lifestyle. The following pages give ideas for using chicken in snacks and salads, as well as soups and main-course meals, exploring its natural versatility.

Braised Chicken with Garlic & Spices, page 82

Soups

Chicken soup is best known as a comforting food, and indeed, thick soups such as Chicken, Sweetcorn & Bean are perfect for warming you up after a walk on a cold winter's day. And chicken soup can be light and nutritious – Chicken and Spring Vegetable Soup will sharpen the appetite of a convalescent, and restore strength. It can also be delicious and elegant. For a soup to begin a Thai meal, Chicken, Leek & Celery is flavoured with coconut milk and nutmeg. Chicken, Avocado & Chipotle Soup combines chicken with spicy Mexican flavours.

Chicken & Rice Soup

1.5 litres/2¾ pints
chicken stock
2 small carrots, very
thinly sliced
1 stick of celery, diced
finely
1 baby leek, halved
lengthways and
sliced thinly
115 g/4 oz petits pois,
defrosted if frozen
75 g/2¾ oz cooked rice
150 g/5½ oz cooked
chicken meat, sliced
2 tsp chopped fresh
tarragon
1 tbsp chopped fresh
parsley
salt and pepper
parsley sprigs, to garnish

 extremely easy

serves 4

15 minutes

35–40 minutes

❶ Pour the stock into a large saucepan and add the carrots, celery and leek. Bring to the boil, reduce the heat to low, and simmer gently, partially covered, for 10 minutes.

❷ Stir in the peas, rice and chicken meat, and continue cooking for 10–15 minutes more, or until the vegetables are tender.

❸ Add the chopped tarragon and parsley, then taste and adjust the seasoning, adding salt and pepper as needed.

❹ Ladle the soup into warm bowls, garnish with sprigs of fresh parsley, and serve.

COOK'S TIP
If the stock you are using is a little weak, or if you have used a stock cube, add the herbs at the beginning, so they can flavour the stock for longer.

Chicken, Sweetcorn & Bean Soup

INGREDIENTS

40 g/1½ oz butter
1 large onion, chopped finely
1 garlic clove, chopped finely
40 g/1½ oz plain flour
600 ml/1 pint water
1 litre/1¾ pints chicken stock
1 carrot, sliced thinly
175 g/6 oz French beans, cut into short pieces
400 g/14 oz canned butter beans, rinsed
350 g/12 oz cooked or frozen sweetcorn kernels
225 g/8 oz cooked chicken meat, cubed
salt and pepper

 extremely easy

 serves 4

 10 minutes

1 hour

❶ Melt the butter in a large saucepan over a medium–low heat. Add the onion and garlic and fry, stirring frequently, for 3–4 minutes, or until just softened.

❷ Stir in the flour and continue cooking for 2 minutes, stirring occasionally.

❸ Gradually pour in the water, stirring constantly and scraping the bottom of the pan to mix in the flour. Bring to the boil, stirring frequently, and cook for 2 minutes. Add the stock and stir until smooth.

❹ Add the carrot, French beans, butter beans, sweetcorn kernals and chicken. Season with salt and pepper. Bring back to the boil, reduce the heat to medium–low, cover, and simmer for 35 minutes, or until the vegetables are tender.

❺ Taste the soup and adjust the seasoning, adding salt, if needed, and plenty of pepper.

❻ Ladle the soup into warm, deep bowls and serve.

VARIATION

Butter beans may be replaced with 300g/10½ oz cooked fresh broad beans, peeled if wished, or flageolet beans, and French beans with sliced runner beans.

Chicken, Leek & Celery Soup

❶ Heat the stock in a saucepan with the bay leaf until the stock is steaming. Add the chicken breast and simmer for 20 minutes, or until firm to the touch. Discard the bay leaf and remove the chicken. When it is cool, cut into small cubes.

❷ Put the flour in a bowl. Very slowly whisk in enough stock to make a smooth liquid, adding about half the stock.

❸ Heat the butter in a saucepan, then add the onion, leeks and half of the celery. Fry for 5 minutes, stirring frequently, until the leeks begin to soften. Pour in the flour and stock mixture slowly, and bring to the boil, stirring constantly. Stir in the remaining stock. Add seasoning, reduce the heat, cover, and simmer for 25 minutes, or until the vegetables are tender.

❹ Allow the soup to cool slightly, then transfer to a blender or a food processor and purée until smooth, working in batches, if necessary. (If using a food processor, strain off the liquid and reserve. Purée the soup solids with a little of the liquid, then combine with the remaining liquid.)

❺ Return the soup to the saucepan and stir in the cream and nutmeg. Season to taste. Place over a medium–low heat. Add the chicken and remaining celery, then simmer for 15 minutes, or until the celery is tender. Serve, sprinkled with coriander.

easy

serves 4

15 minutes, plus 30 minutes to cool

1 hour 10 minutes

Chicken & Spring Vegetable Soup

INGREDIENTS

1 litre/1¾ pints
   chicken stock
175 g/6 oz skinless
   boned chicken breast
fresh parsley and
   tarragon sprigs
2 garlic cloves, crushed
125 g/4½ oz baby carrots,
   halved
225 g/8 oz small new
   potatoes, quartered
55 g/2 oz plain flour
125 ml/4 fl oz milk
4–5 spring onions, sliced
   diagonally
85 g/3 oz asparagus tips,
   halved and cut into
   4 cm/1½ inch pieces
125 ml/4 fl oz whipping
   or double cream
1 tbsp finely chopped
   fresh parsley
1 tbsp finely chopped
   fresh tarragon
salt and pepper

❶ Put the stock in a saucepan with the chicken, parsley and tarragon sprigs and garlic. Bring just to the boil, reduce the heat, cover, and simmer for 20 minutes, or until the chicken is cooked through and firm to the touch.

❷ Remove the chicken and strain the stock. When the chicken is cool enough to handle, cut into bite-sized pieces.

❸ Return the stock to the saucepan and bring to the boil. Adjust the heat so the liquid boils very gently. Add the carrots, then cover and cook for 5 minutes. Put in the potatoes, cover again, and cook for about 12 minutes, or until the vegetables are beginning to become tender.

❹ Meanwhile, put the flour in a small mixing bowl and very slowly whisk in the milk to make a thick paste. Stir in a little of the hot stock mixture to make a smooth liquid.

❺ Stir in the flour mixture and bring just to the boil, stirring. Boil gently for 4–5 minutes until it thickens, stirring frequently.

❻ Add the spring onions, asparagus and chicken. Reduce the heat a little and simmer for about 15 minutes, or until all the vegetables are tender. Stir in the cream and herbs. Season and serve.

 easy

serves 4

 15 minutes

1¼ hours

Chicken & Chickpea Soup with Fruit

800 g/1 lb 12 oz chicken
   legs, skinned
1 stick of celery, sliced
1 large carrot, halved
   and sliced
1 large onion,
   chopped finely
2 garlic cloves, chopped
2.5 litres/4½ pints
   chicken stock
4–5 parsley stalks
1 bay leaf
125 g/4½ oz lean
   smoked ham, diced
400 g/14 oz canned
   chickpeas, rinsed
1 large turnip, diced
2 courgettes, halved
   and sliced
1 large potato, diced
1 sweet potato, diced
175 g/6 oz sweetcorn
   kernels
3 large pears, peeled,
   cored and diced
3 tbsp fresh lime juice
 2 tbsp olive oil
2 unripe bananas, in
   5 mm/ ¼ inch slices
salt and pepper
chopped fresh parsley,
   to garnish

❶ Put the chicken into a 2.5 litre/4½ pint saucepan with the celery, carrot, onion, garlic, stock, parsley stalks and bay leaf. Bring just to the boil over a medium–high heat and skim off any foam that rises to the surface. Reduce the heat and simmer, partially covered, for about 45 minutes, or until the chicken is tender.

❷ Remove the chicken from the stock. When it is cool, remove the meat from the bones, cut into bite-sized pieces, and reserve. Skim the fat from the stock. Discard the parsley stalks and bay leaf.

❸ Bring the stock just to the boil. Add the ham, chickpeas, turnip, courgettes, potato, sweet potato and sweetcorn. Return the meat to the stock. Adjust the heat so the soup simmers gently, and cook, partially covered, for about 30 minutes, or until all the vegetables are tender.

❹ Add the pears and lime juice to the soup and continue cooking for 5 minutes, or until they are barely poached. Season to taste, adding more lime juice if desired.

❺ Heat the oil in a frying pan over a medium–high heat. Fry the bananas until they are golden. Drain on kitchen paper and keep warm. Ladle the soup into bowls and top with fried banana slices, then garnish with parsley.

easy

serves 4

35 minutes

1 hour 35
minutes

Chicken, Avocado & Chipotle Soup

INGREDIENTS

1.5 litres/2¾ pints
chicken stock
2–3 garlic cloves,
chopped finely
1–2 chipotle chillies, cut
into very thin strips
1 avocado
lime or lemon juice, for
tossing
3–5 spring onions,
sliced thinly
350–400 g/12–14 oz
cooked chicken
breast, cut into strips
or torn into shreds
2 tbsp chopped fresh
coriander
1 lime, cut into wedges,
to serve

❶ Place the stock in a pan with the garlic and chipotle chillies and bring to the boil.

❷ Meanwhile, cut the avocado in half around the stone. Twist apart, then remove the stone with a knife. Carefully peel off the skin, dice the flesh, and toss in lime or lemon juice to prevent discoloration.

❸ Arrange the spring onions, chicken, and avocado in the base of 4 soup bowls or in a large serving bowl, and sprinkle the coriander over the top.

❹ Ladle the hot stock over the ingredients and serve with lime wedges and perhaps a handful of tortilla chips.

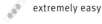

extremely easy

serves 4

15 minutes

10–15 minutes

COOK'S TIP

This dish makes an elegant starter served layered with rounds of tortillas, like a stacked tostada. It also makes a refreshing lunch, served piled in halved avocados, surrounded by sliced mango, papaya, or grapefruit.

18

Cream of Lemon & Chicken with Spaghetti

60 g/2¼ oz butter
8 shallots, sliced thinly
2 carrots, sliced thinly
2 celery sticks,
    sliced thinly
225 g/8 oz boned
    chicken breasts,
    chopped finely
3 lemons
1.2 litres/2 pints chicken
    stock
225 g/8 oz dried
    spaghetti
150 ml/5 fl oz double
    cream
salt and white pepper

GARNISH
fresh parsley sprig
3 lemon slices, halved

 very easy

serves 4

 15 minutes

1¼ hours

❶ Melt the butter in a large saucepan. Add the shallots, carrots, celery and chicken and fry over a low heat, stirring occasionally, for 8 minutes.

❷ Pare the lemons thinly and blanch the lemon rind in boiling water for 3 minutes. Squeeze the juice from the lemons.

❸ Add the lemon rind and juice to the pan, together with the chicken stock. Bring slowly to the boil over a low heat and simmer for 40 minutes.

❹ Add the spaghetti to the pan, breaking it into small pieces as you do so, and cook for 15 minutes. Season to taste with salt and white pepper and add the cream. Heat through, but do not allow the soup to boil or it will curdle.

❺ Pour the soup into a tureen or individual bowls. Garnish the tureen or each dish with the parsley and half slices of lemon, and serve the soup immediately.

COOK'S TIP
You can prepare this soup up to the end of step 3 in advance. Heat the soup through 20 minutes before serving, add the pasta, and complete steps 4 and 5.

Cream of Chicken & Tomato Soup

INGREDIENTS

INGREDIENTS

60 g/2¼ oz unsalted
   butter
1 large onion, chopped
500 g/1 lb 2 oz chicken,
   shredded very finely
600 ml/1 pint chicken
   stock
6 medium tomatoes,
   chopped finely
pinch of bicarbonate
   of soda
1 tbsp caster sugar
150 ml/ 5 fl oz double
   cream
salt and pepper
fresh basil leaves,
   to garnish
croûtons, to serve

❶ Melt the butter in a large saucepan and fry the onion and shredded chicken for 5 minutes.

❷ Add 300 ml/10 fl oz chicken stock to the pan, with the tomatoes and bicarbonate of soda.

❸ Bring the soup to the boil and simmer for 20 minutes.

❹ Allow the soup to cool, then blend in a food processor.

❺ Return the soup to the pan, add the remaining chicken stock, season and add the sugar. Pour the soup into a tureen and add a swirl of double cream. Serve the soup with croûtons and garnish with basil.

very easy

serves 4

15 minutes

40 minutes

COOK'S TIP
For a healthier version
of this soup, use single
cream instead of the
double cream, and omit
the sugar.

Light Meals & Salads

Chicken is an international food, so these pages contain plenty of ideas for turning even a light lunch or supper dish into something special. If you love Mexican food, try Chicken Tostadas – layered beans, cheese, chicken and salad served on a crisp corn tortilla and topped with dried chillies. Indonesian Potato & Chicken Salad is an unusual combination of chicken with vegetables, pineapple and peanuts in a spicy peanut butter dressing. The chapter ends in Italy with a Chicken Risotto à la Milanese.

Chicken & Mushroom Soup with a Puff Pastry Top

INGREDIENTS

1.4 litres/2½ pints stock
4 skinless boned
  chicken breasts
2 garlic cloves, crushed
small bunch of fresh
  tarragon or
  ¼ tsp dried tarragon
15 g/½ oz butter
400 g/14 oz chestnut or
  porcini mushrooms,
  sliced
3 tbsp dry white wine
85 g/3 oz plain flour
175 ml/6 fl oz whipping
  or heavy cream
390 g/13½ oz puff
  pastry
2 tbsp finely chopped
  fresh parsley
salt and pepper

❶ Pour the stock into a pan and bring it to the boil. Add the chicken, garlic and tarragon, reduce the heat, cover, and simmer for 20 minutes, or until cooked through. Remove the chicken and when it is cool, cut it into cubes. Strain the stock.

❷ Melt the butter in a frying pan over a medium heat, then add the mushrooms and seasoning. Fry for 5–8 minutes, or until golden brown, stirring constantly. Add the wine and bubble briefly, then remove from the heat.

❸ Put the flour in a bowl and whisk in the cream to make a thick paste. Stir in some stock to make a smooth liquid. Bring the remaining stock to the boil in a saucepan. Whisk in the flour mixture, then boil gently for 3–4 minutes, or until the soup thickens, stirring often. Add the mushrooms and liquid, if any. Reduce the heat and simmer gently, just to keep warm.

❹ Cut out 6 pastry rounds smaller than the soup bowls. Put on a baking sheet, prick with a fork, and bake in a preheated oven at 200°C/400°F/Gas Mark 6 for 15 minutes, or until golden.

❺ Meanwhile, add the chicken to the soup, season, simmer for about 10 minutes, and stir in the parsley. Ladle the soup into bowls, place the pastry rounds on top, and serve.

easy

serves 4

15 minutes

50 minutes

Wild Rice & Smoked Chicken Chowder

INGREDIENTS

100 g / 3½ oz wild rice, washed
3 fresh ears of corn-on-the-cob, husks and silks removed
2 tbsp vegetable oil
1 large onion, chopped finely
1 celery stick, sliced thinly
1 leek, trimmed and sliced thinly
½ tsp dried thyme
25 g / 1 oz plain flour
3.5 litres / 6¼ pints chicken stock
250 g / 9 oz boned smoked chicken, skinned, diced, or shredded
225 ml / 8 fl oz double or whipping cream
1 tbsp chopped fresh dill
salt and pepper
fresh dill sprigs, to garnish

❶ Bring a large saucepan of water to the boil. Add 1 tablespoon of salt and sprinkle in the wild rice. Return to the boil, then reduce the heat and simmer, covered, for about 40 minutes, or until tender but still firm to the bite. Do not overcook the rice as it will continue to cook in the soup. Drain and rinse, then set aside.

❷ Hold the corn cobs vertical to a chopping board and, using a sharp heavy knife, cut down along the cobs to remove the kernels. Set aside the kernels. Scrape the cob to remove the milky juices and reserve them for the soup.

❸ Heat the oil in a large pan, then add the onion, celery, leek and dried thyme. Fry, stirring frequently, for about 8 minutes, or until the vegetables are very soft.

❹ Sprinkle the flour over the vegetables and stir until blended. Gradually whisk in the stock, add the corn with any juices, and bring to the boil, skimming off any foam. Reduce the heat and simmer for 25 minutes, or until the vegetables are soft and tender.

❺ Stir in the smoked chicken, wild rice, cream and dill, and season to taste. Simmer for 10 minutes, or until the chicken and rice are heated. Garnish with dill sprigs and serve.

 very easy

 serves 4

 15 minutes

 1 hour

Chicken & Sausage Gumbo

INGREDIENTS

1.25 kg/2 lb 12 oz chicken
115 g/4 oz plain flour
175 ml/6 fl oz vegetable
   oil
700 g/1 lb 9 oz andouille
   or other smoked pork
   sausage, cut into
   5 cm/2 inch pieces
2 large onions, chopped
3–4 sticks of celery,
   chopped finely
2 green peppers, cored
   and chopped finely
700 g/1 lb 9 oz okra,
   stems cut into 1 cm/
   ½ inch pieces
4 garlic cloves, chopped
2 bay leaves
½ tsp cayenne pepper
1 tsp black pepper
1 tsp mustard powder
1 tsp dried thyme
½ tsp ground cumin
½ tsp dried oregano
1.5 litres/2¾ pints
   chicken stock,
   simmering
3–4 tomatoes, deseeded
   and chopped
salt
400 g/14 oz cooked
   long-grain white rice,
   to serve

❶ Cut the chicken into 8 pieces and toss it in 2 tablespoons of flour. Heat 2 tablespoons of the oil in a frying pan. Add the chicken and fry for 10 minutes, or until golden. Set aside.

❷ Add the sausage pieces to the pan, stirring and tossing, for about 5 minutes, or until they begin to colour. Set aside.

❸ Heat the remaining oil in the cleaned pan until it begins to smoke. Add all the remaining flour at once and whisk it into the oil. Reduce the heat and cook, stirring frequently, for 20 minutes, or until the roux is a rich brown.

❹ Add the onions, celery and peppers to the roux, and fry, stirring frequently until they begin to soften. Stir in the okra, garlic, bay leaves, cayenne pepper, black pepper, mustard powder, thyme, cumin and oregano, and stir well.

❺ Whisk the hot stock into the mixture little by little, stirring well after each addition. Simmer for about 10 minutes. Stir in the reserved sausage, tomatoes and the chicken, and simmer for 20 minutes, or until the meat is tender.

❻ To serve, fill a cup with rice, packing it lightly, then unmould it into the centre of a wide soup bowl. Spoon the gumbo around the rice at once, and serve.

 very easy

 serves 4

 20 minutes

 1½ hours

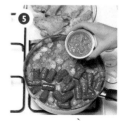

Pad Thai

INGREDIENTS

225 g/8 oz flat rice
noodles (sen lek)
2 tbsp groundnut oil
225 g/8 oz boneless
chicken breasts,
skinned and sliced
4 shallots, chopped
2 garlic cloves, chopped
4 spring onions, cut on
the diagonal into
5 cm/2 inch pieces
350 g/12 oz fresh white
crab meat
125 g/4½ oz fresh bean
sprouts, rinsed
1 tbsp preserved or
fresh radish, diced
2–4 tbsp roasted
peanuts, chopped
fresh coriander sprigs,
to garnish

SAUCE
3 tbsp Thai fish sauce
2–3 tbsp rice vinegar
1 tbsp chilli bean sauce
or oyster sauce
1 tbsp toasted
sesame oil
1 tbsp palm sugar or
light brown sugar
½ tsp cayenne pepper

1 To make the sauce, whisk together the sauce ingredients in a small bowl and set aside.

2 Put the rice noodles in a large bowl and pour enough hot water over to cover them. Leave them to stand for 15 minutes, or until softened. Drain, rinse, and drain again.

3 Heat the oil in a heavy-based wok over a high heat until very hot, but not smoking. Add the chicken strips and stir-fry for 1–2 minutes, or until they just begin to colour. Using a slotted spoon, transfer them to a plate. Reduce the heat to medium–high.

4 Stir the shallots, garlic and spring onions into the wok and stir-fry for about 1 minute. Stir in the drained noodles, then the prepared sauce.

5 Return the reserved chicken to the pan with the crab meat, bean sprouts and radish. Toss well. Cook for about 5 minutes, or until heated through, tossing frequently. If the noodles begin to stick, add a little water.

6 Turn into a serving dish and sprinkle with the chopped peanuts. Garnish with coriander and serve immediately.

 extremely easy

 serves 4

 15 minutes,
plus 15 minutes
to stand

 10 minutes

Pozole

INGREDIENTS

450 g / 1 lb pork for
  stewing, such as
  lean belly
½ small chicken
2 litres / 3½ pints water
1 chicken stock cube
1 whole garlic bulb,
  divided into cloves
  but not peeled
1 onion, chopped
2 bay leaves
450 g / 1 lb cooked
  hominy
¼–½ tsp ground cumin
salt and pepper

TO SERVE
½ small to medium-
  sized cabbage,
  sliced thinly
dried oregano leaves
dried chilli flakes
tortilla chips
lime wedges

❶ Place the pork and chicken in a large pan. Add enough water to fill the pan. (Do not worry about having too much stock, since it keeps fresh up to a week, and freezes well.)

❷ Bring to the boil, then skim off the fat that rises to the surface. Reduce the heat and add the stock cube, garlic, onion and bay leaves. Simmer, covered, over a medium–low heat until the pork and chicken are tender and are cooked through.

❸ Remove the pork and chicken from the soup and leave to cool. When cool enough to handle, remove the chicken flesh from the bones and cut the pork into bite-sized pieces. Set aside.

❹ Skim the fat off the soup and discard the bay leaves. Add the hominy and cumin, salt and pepper to taste. Bring to the boil.

❺ To serve, place a little pork and chicken in soup bowls. Top with cabbage, oregano and chilli flakes, then spoon hot soup into the bowls. Serve with tortilla chips and lime.

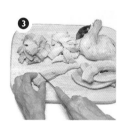

 very easy

 serves 4

 15 minutes

40 minutes

Chicken Tacos from Puebla

INGREDIENTS

8 soft corn tortillas
2 tsp vegetable oil
225–350 g/8–12 oz left-
    over cooked chicken,
    diced or shredded
225 g/8 oz canned
    refried beans, warmed
    and thinned with
    2 tbsp water
¼ tsp ground cumin
¼ tsp dried oregano
1 avocado, stoned, sliced
    and tossed with
    lime juice
salsa verde or other
    salsa of your choice
1 canned chipotle chilli in
    adobo marinade,
    chopped, or bottled
    chipotle salsa
¾ cup soured cream
½ onion, chopped
handful of lettuce leaves
5 radishes, diced
salt and pepper

❶ Warm a frying pan on a medium heat and stack the tortillas in it in to heat. Alternate the top and bottom tortillas so that the stack heats evenly. Wrap the heated tortillas in foil or a clean tea towel to keep warm.

❷ Heat the oil in a frying pan, then add the chicken and heat through. Season with salt and pepper to taste.

❸ Combine the refried beans with the cumin and oregano.

❹ Spread one tortilla with warm refried beans, then top with a spoonful of the chicken, a slice or two of avocado, a dab of salsa, chipotle to taste, a dollop of soured cream, and a sprinkling of onion, lettuce and radishes. Season with salt and pepper to taste, then roll up. Repeat with the remaining tortillas and serve at once.

 extremely easy

 serves 4

 20 minutes

 20 minutes

Chicken Tostadas with Green Salsa & Chipotle

INGREDIENTS

vegetable oil, for frying
6 soft corn tortillas
450 g/1 lb skinned
  boned chicken breast
  or thigh, cut into strips
  or small pieces
225 ml/8 fl oz chicken
  stock
2 garlic cloves,
  chopped finely
400 g/14 oz refried beans
large pinch of ground
  cumin
225 g/8 oz grated cheese
1 tbsp chopped fresh
  coriander
2 ripe tomatoes, diced
handful of crisp lettuce
  leaves, such as cos
  or iceberg, shredded
4–6 radishes, diced
3 spring onions,
  sliced thinly
1 ripe avocado, pitted,
  diced or sliced and
  tossed with lime juice
soured cream, to taste
1–2 canned chipotle
  chillies in adobo
  marinade, or dried
  chipotle reconstituted,
  cut into thin strips

❶ To make tostadas, fry the tortillas in a small amount of oil in a non-stick pan until crisp.

❷ Put the chicken in a pan with the stock and garlic. Bring to the boil, then reduce the heat and cook for 1–2 minutes, or until the chicken begins to turn opaque.

❸ Remove the chicken from the heat and leave it to steep in the hot liquid to cook through.

❹ Heat the beans with enough water to form a smooth purée. Add the cumin and keep warm.

❺ Reheat the tostadas under a preheated grill, if necessary. Spread the hot beans on the tostadas, then sprinkle with the grated cheese. Lift the cooked chicken from the liquid and divide between the tostadas. Sprinkle with the coriander and top with the tomatoes, lettuce, radishes, spring onions, avocado, soured cream and a few strips of chipotle. Serve immediately.

 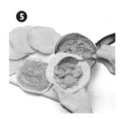 

 extremely easy

 serves 4

 20 minutes

 20 minutes

Green Chilli & Chicken Chilaquiles

INGREDIENTS

12 stale tortillas, cut into strips
1 tbsp vegetable oil
1 small cooked chicken, meat removed from the bones and cut into bite-sized pieces
salsa verde
8 tbsp chopped fresh coriander
1 tsp finely chopped fresh oregano or thyme
4 garlic cloves, chopped finely
¼ tsp ground cumin
350 g/12 oz grated cheese, such as Cheddar, manchego or mozzarella
450 ml/16 fl oz chicken stock
125 g/4½ oz freshly grated Parmesan cheese

TO SERVE
350 ml/12 fl oz crème fraîche or soured cream
3–5 spring onions, sliced thinly
pickled chillies

❶ Place the tortilla strips in a roasting tin, toss with the oil and bake in a preheated oven at 190°C/375°F/Gas Mark 5 for about 30 minutes, or until they are crisp and golden.

❷ Arrange the chicken in a 22.5 × 32.5 cm/9 × 13 inch casserole, then sprinkle with half the salsa verde and the coriander, oregano, garlic, cumin and cheese. Repeat these layers and top with the tortilla strips.

❸ Pour the stock over the top, then sprinkle with the remaining cheeses.

❹ Bake in a preheated oven at 190°C/375°F/Gas Mark 5 for 30 minutes, or until the cheese is lightly golden in areas.

❺ Garnish with the crème fraîche, spring onions and pickled chillies. Serve the chilaquiles at once.

 extremely easy

serves 4

15 minutes

1 hour

Lemon Grass Chicken Skewers

2 long or 4 short lemon grass stalks
2 large boneless, skinless chicken breasts, about 400 g / 14 oz in total
1 small egg white
1 carrot, grated finely
1 small red chilli, deseeded and chopped
2 tbsp chopped fresh garlic chives
2 tbsp chopped fresh coriander
1 tbsp sunflower oil
salt and pepper
coriander and lime slices, to garnish

very easy

serves 4

15 minutes, plus 15 minutes to chill

4–6 minutes

❶ If the lemon grass stalks are long, cut them in half across the middle to make 4 short lengths. Cut each stalk in half lengthways, so you have 8 sticks.

❷ Chop the chicken pieces roughly and place them in a food processor with the egg white. Process to a smooth paste, then add the carrot, chilli, chives, coriander, and salt and pepper. Process for a few seconds to mix well.

❸ Chill the mixture in the refrigerator for about 15 minutes. Divide the mixture into 8 equal portions, and use your hands to shape the mixture around the skewers fashioned from lemon grass.

❹ Brush the skewers with oil and grill them under a preheated medium–hot grill for 4–6 minutes, turning them occasionally, until they are golden brown and cooked thoroughly. Alternatively, grill over medium–hot coals.

❺ Serve hot, with coriander and lime slices to garnish.

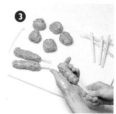

COOK'S TIP
If whole lemon-grass stalks are not available, use wooden or bamboo skewers and add ½ teaspoon ground lemon grass to the mixture with the other flavourings.

Chicken Balls with Dipping Sauce

INGREDIENTS

2 large boneless,
skinless chicken
breasts
3 tbsp vegetable oil
2 shallots, chopped
finely
½ celery stick, chopped
finely
1 garlic clove, crushed
2 tbsp light soy sauce
1 small egg
1 bunch spring onions
salt and pepper
spring onion tassels,
to garnish

DIPPING SAUCE
3 tbsp dark soy sauce
1 tbsp rice wine
1 tsp sesame seeds

❶ Cut the chicken into 2 cm/¾ inch pieces. Heat half of the oil in a wok and stir-fry the chicken quickly over a high heat for 2–3 minutes, or until golden. Remove the chicken from the wok with a perforated spoon and set aside.

❷ Add the shallots, celery and garlic to the wok and stir-fry for 1–2 minutes, or until softened but not browned.

❸ Place the chicken, shallots, celery and garlic in a food processor and process until they are minced finely. Add 1 tablespoon of the light soy sauce and salt and pepper, and just enough egg to make a fairly firm mixture.

❹ Trim the spring onions and cut into 5 cm/2 inch lengths. Make the dipping sauce by mixing together the dark soy sauce, rice wine and sesame seeds. Set aside.

❺ Shape the chicken mixture into 16–18 walnut-sized balls. Heat the remaining oil in a wok, and stir-fry the chicken balls in small batches for 4–5 minutes, or until golden brown. Drain on kitchen paper and keep hot.

❻ Stir-fry the spring onions for 1–2 minutes to soften, then stir in the remaining light soy sauce. Serve with the chicken balls and dipping sauce. Serve on a plate, garnished with spring onion tassels.

 easy

 serves 4

 15 minutes

 about 30 minutes

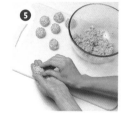

Rice Noodles with Chicken & Pak Choi

INGREDIENTS

200 g/7 oz rice stick
noodles
1 tbsp sunflower oil
1 garlic clove, chopped
finely
2 cm/¾ inch piece
fresh ginger,
chopped finely
4 spring onions,
chopped
1 red bird's eye chilli,
deseeded and sliced
300 g/10½ oz boneless,
skinless chicken,
chopped finely
2 chicken livers,
chopped finely
1 stick of celery,
sliced thinly
1 carrot, cut into fine
matchsticks
300 g/10½ oz shredded
pak choi
4 tbsp lime juice
2 tbsp Thai fish sauce
1 tbsp soy sauce

TO GARNISH
2 tbsp fresh chopped
mint
slices of pickled garlic

 extremely easy

 serves 4

 15 minutes,
plus 15 minutes
to soak

10 minutes

❶ Soak the rice noodles in hot water for 15 minutes, or according to the package directions. Drain well.

❷ Heat the oil in a wok and stir-fry the garlic, ginger, spring onions and chilli for about 1 minute. Stir in the chicken and chicken livers, then stir-fry over a high heat for 2–3 minutes, or until just beginning to brown.

❸ Stir in the celery and carrot and stir-fry for a further 2 minutes to soften. Add the pak choi, then stir in the lime juice, fish sauce, and soy sauce.

❹ Add the noodles and stir to heat thoroughly. Sprinkle with mint and pickled garlic. Serve immediately.

Indonesian Potato & Chicken Salad

INGREDIENTS

4 large waxy potatoes, diced
300 g/10½ oz fresh pineapple, diced, or canned unsweetened pineapple chunks
2 carrots, grated
175 g/6 oz beansprouts
1 bunch spring onions, sliced
1 large courgette, cut into matchsticks
3 sticks of celery, cut into matchsticks
175 g/6 oz unsalted peanuts
2 cooked chicken breasts, about 125 g/ 4½ oz each, sliced
lime wedges, to garnish

DRESSING
6 tbsp crunchy peanut butter
6 tbsp olive oil
2 tbsp light soy sauce
1 red chilli, chopped
2 tsp sesame oil
4 tsp lime juice

❶ Cook the diced potatoes in a pan of boiling water for 10 minutes, or until tender. Drain and leave to cool.

❷ Transfer the cooled potatoes to a salad bowl.

❸ Add to the potatoes the diced fresh pineapple, or the canned pineapple chunks, drained and rinsed in cold running water, the carrots, beansprouts, spring onions, courgette, celery, peanuts and sliced chicken. Toss well to combine all the ingredients.

❹ To make the dressing, put the peanut butter in a small bowl and gradually whisk in the olive oil and soy sauce.

❺ Stir in the chopped red chilli, sesame oil and lime juice. Mix until well combined.

❻ Pour the spicy dressing over the salad and toss lightly to coat all the ingredients. Serve the salad immediately, garnished with the lime wedges.

 extremely easy

 serves 4

 20 minutes

 10 minutes

Potato, Chicken & Banana Cake

INGREDIENTS

450 g/1 lb floury
  potatoes, diced
225 g/8 oz minced
  chicken
1 large banana
25 g/1 oz plain flour
1 tsp lemon juice
1 onion, chopped finely
2 tbsp chopped fresh
  sage
25 g/1 oz butter
2 tbsp vegetable oil
150 ml/5 fl oz single
  cream
150 ml/5 fl oz chicken
  stock
salt and pepper
fresh sage leaves,
  to garnish

easy

serves 4

20 minutes

45 minutes

COOK'S TIP
Do not boil the sauce
after the cream has
been added in step 5,
or it will curdle. Instead,
cook the sauce gently
over a very low heat.

❶ Cook the diced potatoes in a saucepan of boiling water for 10 minutes, or until cooked. Drain the potatoes and mash them until smooth. Stir in the chicken.

❷ Mash the banana and add it to the potato with the flour, lemon juice, onion and half of the chopped sage. Season well and stir the mixture.

❸ Divide the mixture into 8 equal portions. With lightly floured hands, shape each portion into a round patty.

❹ Heat the butter and oil in a frying pan, add the potato cakes, and fry for 12–15 minutes, or until cooked through, turning once. Remove from the pan and keep warm.

❺ Stir the cream and stock into the pan with the remaining chopped sage. Cook over a low heat for 2–3 minutes.

❻ Arrange the potato cakes on a serving plate, garnish them with fresh sage leaves, and serve them hot with the cream and sage sauce.

Chicken Risotto à la Milanese

INGREDIENTS

125 g/4½ oz butter
900 g/2 lb chicken
meat, sliced thinly
1 large onion, chopped
500 g/1 lb 2 oz arborio
rice
600 ml/1 pint chicken
stock
150 ml/5 fl oz white
wine
1 tsp crumbled saffron
salt and pepper
60 g/2¼ oz grated
Parmesan cheese,
to serve

❶ Heat 60 g/2¼ oz of butter in a deep frying pan, and fry the chicken and onion until golden brown.

❷ Add the rice, stir well, and cook for 15 minutes.

❸ Heat the stock until it is boiling and add it, little by little, to the rice. Add the white wine, saffron, and salt and pepper to taste, and mix well. Simmer gently for 20 minutes, stirring occasionally, and adding more stock if the risotto becomes too dry.

❹ Leave to stand for a few minutes and just before serving add a little more stock and simmer for another 10 minutes. Serve the risotto, sprinkled with the grated Parmesan cheese and the remaining butter.

 extremely easy

 serves 4

 10 minutes, plus 5 minutes to stand

 45 minutes

COOK'S TIP
A risotto should have moist but separate grains. Stock should be added a ladleful at a time, and only when the last addition has been absorbed completely.

Main Meals

Chicken works well cooked with other meats and even with seafood to make hearty main-course dishes. The classic Spanish Paella is packed with exciting tastes, textures and flavours: chicken, chorizo sausage and ham are buried with prawns, clams and mussels in short-grain rice flavoured with saffron. Moroccan Chicken Couscous is an exotic dish of chicken with vegetables, pulses, fruits and spices, resting on a bed of couscous. Chicken with Green Olives & Pasta is an uncomplicated, tasty dish of chicken casseroled with vegetables in a wine and cream sauce.

Spanish Chicken with Garlic

INGREDIENTS

25–40 g/1–1½ oz plain
  flour
cayenne pepper
4 chicken quarters
  or other joints,
  patted dry
about 4 tbsp olive oil
20 large garlic cloves,
  each halved, green
  core removed
1 large bay leaf
450 ml/16 fl oz chicken
  stock
4 tbsp dry white wine
chopped fresh parsley,
  to garnish
salt and pepper

 very easy

 serves 4

 10 minutes

1 hour

❶ Put about 2 tablespoons of the flour in a plastic bag and season to taste with cayenne pepper and salt and pepper. Add a chicken piece and shake until it is lightly coated with the flour, shaking off the excess. Repeat with the remaining pieces, adding more flour and seasoning as necessary.

❷ Heat 3 tablespoons of olive oil in a frying pan. Add the garlic cloves and fry for 2 minutes, stirring, to flavour the oil. Remove the garlic with a slotted spoon and set aside.

❸ Add the chicken to the pan, skin-side down, and fry for 5 minutes, or until golden. Turn and fry for 5 minutes more, adding 1–2 tablespoons oil if necessary to prevent sticking.

❹ Return the garlic to the pan. Add the bay leaf, stock and wine, and bring to the boil, then cover and simmer for 25 minutes, or until the chicken is tender and the garlic cloves are soft. Using a slotted spoon, transfer the chicken to a serving plate, and keep warm. Bring the cooking liquid to the boil with the garlic, and boil until reduced to about 250 ml/9 fl oz. Adjust the seasoning, if necessary.

❺ Spoon the sauce over the chicken pieces and scatter the garlic cloves around. Garnish with parsley and serve.

Moroccan Chicken Couscous

INGREDIENTS

about 3 tbsp olive oil
8 chicken pieces with
bones
2 large onions, chopped
2 large garlic cloves,
crushed
2.5 cm/1 inch piece
ginger root, peeled
and chopped finely
150 g/5½ oz dried
chickpeas, soaked
overnight and drained
4 large carrots, cut into
thick chunks
large pinch of saffron
threads, dissolved in
2 tbsp boiling water
grated rind of 2 lemons
2 red peppers, cored
and sliced
2 large courgettes, cut
into chunks
2 tomatoes, deseeded
and chopped
100 g/3½ oz dried
apricots, chopped
½ tsp ground cumin
½ tsp ground coriander
½ tsp cayenne pepper
600 ml/1 pint water
1 tbsp butter
3⅓ cups instant couscous
salt and pepper

❶ Heat 3 tablespoons of the oil in a large flameproof casserole. Pat the chicken pieces dry with kitchen paper, add to the oil, skin-side down, and fry for 5 minutes, or until crisp and brown. Remove from the casserole and set aside.

❷ Add the onions to the casserole, adding a little extra oil, if necessary. Fry the onions for 5 minutes, then add the garlic and ginger and fry for another 2 minutes, stirring occasionally. Return the chicken to the casserole. Add the chickpeas, carrots, saffron and lemon rind. Pour in enough water to cover by 2.5 cm/1 inch and bring to the boil.

❸ Lower the heat, cover, and simmer until the chickpeas are tender. Add the dried apricots, peppers, courgettes, tomatoes, cumin, coriander, cayenne pepper, and salt and pepper to taste. Re-cover and simmer for 15 minutes more.

❹ Meanwhile, bring the water to the boil. Stir in the butter and ½ teaspoon of salt, then sprinkle in the couscous. Cover the pan tightly, remove from the heat and leave it to stand for 10 minutes, or until the grains are tender.

❺ Fluff the couscous with a fork. Taste and adjust the seasoning of the stew. Spoon the couscous into individual bowls and serve the stew in a separate serving bowl.

very easy

serves 4

20 minutes, plus
8 hours to soak

1 hour 25
minutes

Chicken Basquaise

INGREDIENTS

1.3 kg/3 lb chicken,
  cut into 8 pieces
flour, for dusting
2–3 tbsp olive oil
1 large onion, sliced
  thickly
2 peppers, deseeded
  and cut lengthways
  into thick strips
2 garlic cloves
140 g/5 oz spicy chorizo
  sausage, peeled,
  and cut into
  1 cm/½ inch pieces
1 tbsp tomato purée
200 g/7 oz long-grain
  white rice or medium-
  grain Spanish rice,
  such as Valencia
450 ml/16 fl oz chicken
  stock
1 tsp crushed dried
  chillies
½ tsp dried thyme
115 g/4 oz Bayonne or
  other air-dried ham,
  diced
12 dry-cured black
  olives
2 tbsp chopped fresh
  flat-leaved parsley
salt and pepper

❶ Dry the chicken pieces with kitchen paper. Put about 2 tablespoons flour in a plastic bag and season with salt and pepper, then add the chicken pieces. Seal the bag and shake to coat the chicken.

❷ Heat 2 tablespoons of the oil in a large flameproof casserole over medium–high heat. Add the chicken and fry for 15 minutes, or until browned. Transfer to a plate.

❸ Heat the remaining oil in the casserole and add the onion and peppers. Reduce the heat to medium and stir-fry until they begin to colour and soften. Add the garlic, chorizo and tomato purée, and continue stirring for about 3 minutes. Add the rice and cook for about 2 minutes, stirring to coat, until the rice is translucent.

❹ Add the stock, crushed chillies, thyme, and salt and pepper and stir. Bring to the boil. Return the chicken to the casserole, pressing gently into the rice. Cover and cook over very low heat for about 45 minutes, or until the chicken and rice are tender.

❺ Stir the ham, black olives and half the parsley gently into the rice mixture. Re-cover and heat for 5 minutes more. Sprinkle with the remaining parsley, and serve.

 very easy

 serves 4

 10 minutes

1½ hours

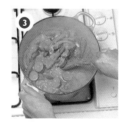

Poussins with a Fruity Rice Stuffing

INGREDIENTS

4 Cornish game or other free-range hens
55–85 g/2–3 oz butter

STUFFING
225 ml/8 fl oz port
150 g/5½ oz raisins
1 cup dried no-soak apricots, sliced
2–3 tbsp extra-virgin olive oil
1 onion, chopped finely
1 stick of celery, sliced
2 garlic cloves, chopped
1 tsp ground cinnamon
1 tsp dried oregano
1 tsp dried mint or basil
½ tsp mixed spice
225 g/8 oz unsweetened chestnuts
75 g/2¾ oz long-grain white rice, cooked
grated rind and juice of 2 oranges
350 ml/12 fl oz chicken stock
55 g/2 oz walnuts, lightly toasted and chopped
2 tbsp chopped fresh mint
2 tbsp chopped fresh flat-leaved parsley
salt and pepper

 easy

 serves 4

 20 minutes, plus 15 minutes to stand

55 minutes, plus 5 minutes to stand

❶ To make the stuffing, combine the port, raisins and apricots in a small bowl and leave to stand for 15 minutes.

❷ Heat the oil in a heavy pan. Add the onion and celery, and cook for 3–4 minutes. Add the garlic, herbs, spices, and chestnuts, and cook for 4 minutes, stirring occasionally. Add the rice and half the orange rind and juice, and the stock. Simmer until most of the liquid is absorbed.

❸ Drain the raisins and apricots, reserving the port, and stir into the rice mixture with the walnuts, mint and parsley, and cook for another 2 minutes. Season with salt and pepper, then remove from the heat and cool.

❹ Rub the hens inside and out with salt and pepper. Fill the cavity of each bird with stuffing, but do not pack too tightly. Tie the legs of each bird together, tucking in the tail. Form extra stuffing into balls. Arrange the birds in a roasting tin with any stuffing balls, and brush with melted butter. Drizzle any remaining butter around the tin. Pour the remaining orange rind and juice, and the reserved port, over the chicken.

❺ Roast in a preheated oven at 180°C/350°F/Gas Mark 4 for 45 minutes, basting, until cooked. Transfer to a plate, cover with foil, and stand for 5 minutes. Serve with any tin juices.

Spanish Paella

INGREDIENTS

125 ml/4 fl oz olive oil
1.5 kg/3 lb 5 oz chicken,
  cut into 8 pieces
350 g/12 oz chorizo
  sausage, cut into
  1 cm/ ½ inch pieces
115 g/4 oz cured ham,
  chopped
2 onions, chopped
2 red peppers, cored
  and cut into 2.5 cm/
  1 inch pieces
4–6 garlic cloves
800 g/1 lb 12 oz short-
  grain Spanish rice or
  Italian arborio rice
2 bay leaves
1 tsp dried thyme
1 tsp saffron threads,
  crushed lightly
225 ml/8 fl oz dry white
  wine
1.5 litres/2¾ pints
  chicken stock
115 g/4 oz peas
450 g/1 lb medium
  uncooked prawns
8 raw king prawns,
  in shells
16 clams, scrubbed
16 mussels, scrubbed
salt and pepper
4 tbsp parsley, chopped

❶ Heat half the oil in an 18 inch/46 cm paella pan or deep, wide frying pan, then add the chicken and fry gently, turning, until golden brown. Remove from the pan and set aside.

❷ Add the chorizo and ham, and fry for 7 minutes, stirring occasionally, until crisp. Remove and set aside.

❸ Stir the onions into the pan and cook for 3 minutes, or until soft. Add the peppers and garlic and cook until they begin to soften. Remove and set aside.

❹ Add the remaining oil to the pan and stir in the rice to coat it. Add the bay leaves, thyme and saffron, and stir. Pour in the wine, simmer, then pour in the stock, scraping the bottom of the pan to stir it in. Bring to the boil, stirring often.

❺ Stir in the chorizo, ham and chicken with the cooked vegetables, and bury them in the rice. Reduce the heat and cook for 10 minutes, stirring occasionally. Add the peas and prawns, and cook for another 5 minutes. Push the clams and mussels into the rice. Cover, and cook gently for about 5 minutes, or until the rice is tender and the shellfish open. Discard any unopened clams or mussels. Season to taste.

❻ Remove from the heat and leave to stand, covered, for about 5 minutes. Sprinkle with chopped parsley and serve.

 easy

 serves 4

 15 minutes,
plus 5 minutes
to stand

 1 hour

Murgh Pullau

INGREDIENTS

*350 g/12 oz basmati
  rice*
4 tbsp ghee or butter
*115 g/4 oz flaked
  almonds*
*115 g/4 oz unsalted,
  shelled pistachio nuts*
*4–6 boned chicken
  breasts, skinned and
  each cut into 4 pieces*
2 onions, sliced thinly
*2 garlic cloves, chopped
  finely*
*2.5 cm/1 inch piece
  fresh ginger root,
  peeled and chopped*
*6 green cardamom pods,
  lightly crushed*
4–6 whole cloves
2 bay leaves
1 tsp ground coriander
½ tsp cayenne pepper
*225 ml/8 fl oz natural
  yogurt*
*225 ml/8 fl oz double
  cream*
*2–4 tbsp chopped fresh
  coriander or mint*
*225 g/8 oz seedless
  green grapes, halved
  if large*

❶ Bring a pan of salted water to the boil. Gradually pour in the rice, return to the boil, then simmer until the rice is just tender. Drain and rinse under cold running water. Set aside.

❷ Heat the ghee in a deep frying pan over medium–high heat. Add the almonds and pistachios, and cook for 3 minutes, stirring, until light golden. Remove and reserve.

❸ Add the chicken to the pan and cook for 5 minutes, or until golden, turning. Remove and reserve. Add the onions to the pan. Cook for about 10 minutes, or until golden. Stir in the garlic, herbs and spices, and cook for 3 minutes.

❹ Add 2–3 tablespoons of the yogurt, and cook, stirring, until all the moisture evaporates. Continue adding the rest of the yogurt in the same way.

❺ Return the chicken and nuts to the pan, and stir to coat. Stir in 125 ml/4 fl oz boiling water. Season with salt and pepper. Cover the pan and cook over a low heat for about 10 minutes, or until the chicken is cooked thoroughly. Stir in the cream, coriander and grapes, and remove the pan from the heat.

❻ Fork the rice into a bowl. Gently fold in the chicken and sauce. Leave to stand for 5 minutes, then serve.

 very easy

 serves 4

 10 minutes, plus 5 minutes to stand

 1 hour

Singapore Noodles

55 g/2 oz dried Chinese
mushrooms
225 g/8 oz rice
vermicelli noodles
2–3 tbsp groundnut oil
6–8 garlic cloves,
sliced thinly
2–3 shallots, sliced thinly
2.5 cm/1 inch piece fresh
ginger root, peeled
and sliced thinly
4–5 fresh red chillies,
trimmed, deseeded
and sliced thinly on
the diagonal
225 g/8 oz chicken
breast fillets,
sliced thinly
225 g/8 oz mangetouts,
sliced thinly on the
diagonal
225 g/8 oz Chinese
leaves, thinly
shredded
225 g/8 oz cooked
peeled prawns
6–8 water chestnuts,
sliced
2 spring onions, sliced
thinly on the diagonal
2 tbsp chopped fresh
coriander or mint

❶ To make the curry sauce, whisk the rice wine and soy sauce into the curry powder, then stir in the remaining ingredients.

❷ Put the Chinese mushrooms in a small bowl, and add enough boiling water to cover. Soak for about 15 minutes until softened. Lift out the mushrooms and squeeze out the liquid. Discard any stems, then slice thinly and set aside. Soak the rice noodles according to the instructions on the package, then drain well.

❸ Heat the oil in a wok or a deep frying pan over a medium–high heat. Add the garlic, shallots, ginger and chillies, and stir-fry for about 30 seconds. Add the chicken and mangetouts, and stir-fry for about 2 minutes. Add the Chinese leaves, prawns, water chestnuts, mushrooms and spring onions, and stir-fry for 1–2 minutes. Add the curry sauce and noodles, and stir-fry for 5 minutes. Sprinkle with fresh coriander, and serve.

 extremely easy

 serves 4

 30 minutes, plus
15 minutes to
soak

 12 minutes

SINGAPORE CURRY SAUCE

2 tbsp rice wine or dry sherry	1 tbsp sugar
2 tbsp soy sauce	400 ml/14 fl oz canned coconut milk
3 tbsp curry powder, medium or hot Madras depending on taste	1 tsp salt
	black pepper, to taste

Simmered Stew of Meat, Chicken, Vegetables & Fruit

INGREDIENTS

900 g / 2 lb piece boneless pork or pork pieces
2 bay leaves
1 onion, chopped
8 garlic cloves, chopped finely
2 tbsp chopped fresh coriander
1 carrot, sliced thinly
2 sticks of celery, diced
2 chicken stock cubes
½ chicken, portioned
4–5 ripe tomatoes, diced
½ tsp mild chilli powder
grated rind of ¼ orange
¼ tsp ground cumin
juice of 3 oranges
1 courgette, cut into bite-sized pieces
¼ cabbage, sliced thinly and blanched
1 apple, peeled, cored and cubed
about 10 prunes, stoned
¼ tsp ground cinnamon
pinch of dried ginger
350 g / 12 oz chorizo sausage, diced
salt and pepper

❶ Combine the pork, bay leaves, onion, garlic, coriander, carrot and celery in a large saucepan and fill with cold water to the top. Bring to the boil, skim off the scum that has formed on the surface, then reduce the heat and simmer gently for an hour.

❷ Add the stock cubes to the saucepan, along with the chicken, tomatoes, chilli powder, orange rind and cumin. Continue to cook for a further 45 minutes, or until the chicken is tender. Spoon off the fat that forms on the top of the liquid.

❸ Add the orange juice, courgette, cabbage, apple, prunes, cinnamon, ginger and chorizo. Continue to simmer for a further 20 minutes, or until the courgette is tender and the chorizo cooked through.

❹ Season with salt and pepper, and serve at once.

 extremely easy

 serves 4

 20 minutes

 2 hours 20 minutes

Chicken Breasts in Green Salsa with Soured Cream

INGREDIENTS

4 chicken breast fillets
flour, for dredging
55–85 g/2–3 oz butter
or butter and oil
450 g/1 lb mild green
salsa or puréed
tomatillos
225 ml/8 fl oz chicken
stock
1–2 garlic cloves,
chopped finely
3–5 tbsp chopped fresh
coriander
½ fresh green chilli,
deseeded and
chopped
½ tsp ground cumin
salt and pepper

TO SERVE
1 cup soured cream
several leaves cos
lettuce, shredded
3–5 spring onions,
sliced thinly
coarsely chopped fresh
coriander

❶ Sprinkle the chicken with salt and pepper, then dredge in flour. Shake off the excess.

❷ Melt the butter in a frying pan, add the chicken, and fry over a medium–high heat, turning once, until the fillets are golden but not cooked through – they will cook slightly in the sauce. Remove from the pan and set aside.

❸ Place the salsa, chicken stock, garlic, coriander, chilli and cumin in a pan, and bring to the boil. Reduce the heat to a low simmer. Add the chicken breasts to the sauce, spooning the sauce over the chicken. Continue to cook until the chicken is cooked through.

❹ Remove the chicken from the pan and season with salt and pepper. Serve with the soured cream, shredded lettuce, spring onions and fresh coriander leaves.

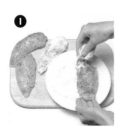

 extremely easy

 serves 4

 15 minutes

 30 minutes

Chicken with Purslane & Red Chilli

INGREDIENTS

juice of 1 lime

6 garlic cloves, chopped finely

¼ tsp dried oregano

¼ tsp dried marjoram

¼ tsp dried thyme

½ tsp ground cumin

1 chicken, cut into 4 pieces

about 10 large dried mild chillies, such as pasilla

450 ml/16 fl oz boiling water

450 ml/16 fl oz chicken stock

3 tbsp extra-virgin olive oil

700 g/1 lb 9 oz tomatoes, charred under the grill, skinned and deseeded

handful of corn tortilla chips, crushed

several large handfuls of purslane, cut into bite-sized lengths

½ lime

salt and pepper

lime wedges, to serve

❶ Combine the lime juice, half the garlic, the oregano, marjoram, thyme, cumin and salt to taste. Rub the mixture over the chicken and leave to marinate for at least an hour, or overnight in the refrigerator.

❷ Place the chillies in a saucepan, and pour the boiling water over them. Cover and leave for 30 minutes. Remove the stems and seeds, and purée the flesh in a blender or a food processor, adding enough stock to make a smooth paste. Add the rest of the stock, mix well, and set aside.

❸ Heat 1 tablespoon of oil in a frying pan. Add the chilli paste with the tomatoes and remaining garlic. Fry over a medium heat, stirring, until reduced by half. Set aside.

❹ Remove the chicken from the marinade, reserving any juices. Brown the chicken pieces in the remaining oil, then place in a flameproof casserole. Add any reserved juices and the reduced chilli sauce. Cover and simmer over a low heat for about 30 minutes, or until the chicken is tender.

❺ Stir the crushed tortillas into the sauce, and cook for a few minutes. Add the purslane. Season the casserole with salt, pepper and a squeeze of lime, and serve garnished with lime wedges.

 very easy

 serves 4

 15 minutes, plus 1 hour to marinate and to stand

 45 minutes

Jambalaya

INGREDIENTS

2 tbsp vegetable oil
2 onions, chopped
  roughly
1 green pepper,
  deseeded and
  chopped roughly
2 celery sticks,
  chopped roughly
3 garlic cloves,
  chopped finely
2 tsp paprika
300 g/10½ oz skinless,
  boneless chicken
  breasts, chopped
100 g/3½ oz boudin
  sausages, chopped
3 tomatoes, skinned
  and chopped
400 g/14 oz long-grain
  rice
850 ml/1½ pints hot
  chicken or fish stock
1 tsp dried oregano
2 fresh bay leaves
12 king prawn tails
4 spring onions,
  chopped finely
2 tbsp chopped fresh
  parsley
salt and pepper
salad, to serve

❶ Heat the vegetable oil in a large frying pan and add the onions, pepper, celery and garlic. Fry for 8–10 minutes, or until all the vegetables have softened. Add the paprika and fry for another 30 seconds. Add the chicken and sausages and cook for 8–10 minutes, or until they are lightly browned. Add the tomatoes and cook for 2–3 minutes, or until they have collapsed.

❷ Add the rice to the pan and stir well. Pour in the hot stock, oregano and bay leaves, and stir well. Cover and simmer for 10 minutes over a very low heat.

❸ Add the prawns and stir well. Cover again and cook for an additional 6–8 minutes, or until the rice is tender and the prawns are cooked through.

❹ Stir in the spring onions and parsley, then season to taste. Serve immediately.

 extremely easy

 serves 4

 15 minutes

 45 minutes

Chicken & Mango Stir-Fry

6 boneless, skinless
  chicken thighs
2.5 cm/1 inch piece
  fresh ginger, grated
1 garlic clove, crushed
1 small red chilli,
  deseeded
1 large red pepper
4 spring onions
150 g/5½ oz
  mangetouts
1 cup baby sweetcorn
1 large firm, ripe mango
2 tbsp sunflower oil
1 tbsp light soy sauce
3 tbsp rice wine or
  sherry
1 tsp sesame oil
salt and pepper

❶ Cut the chicken into long, thin strips and place in a bowl. Mix together the ginger, garlic and chilli, then stir the mixture into the chicken strips to coat them evenly.

❷ Slice the pepper thinly, cutting diagonally. Trim the onions and slice them diagonally. Cut the mangetouts and sweetcorn in half diagonally. Peel the mango, remove the stone, and slice thinly.

❸ Heat the oil in a wok or a frying pan over a high heat. Add the chicken and stir-fry for 4–5 minutes, or until it just turns golden. Add the peppers and stir-fry over a medium heat for 4–5 minutes to soften. Add the spring onions, sweetcorn and mangetouts, and stir-fry for another minute.

❹ Mix together the soy sauce, rice wine or sherry, and sesame oil, and stir it into the wok. Add the mango and stir gently for 1 minute to heat thoroughly. Adjust the seasoning with salt and pepper to taste, and serve immediately.

 extremely easy

 serves 4

 15 minutes

 15 minutes

Green Chicken Curry

INGREDIENTS

*6 boneless, skinless
chicken thighs*
*400 ml/14 fl oz coconut
milk*
2 garlic cloves, crushed
2 tbsp Thai fish sauce
2 tbsp green curry paste
12 baby aubergines
*3 green chillies,
chopped finely*
*3 kaffir lime leaves,
shredded*
*4 tbsp chopped fresh
coriander*
boiled rice, to serve

❶ Cut the chicken into bite-sized pieces. Pour the coconut milk into a wok or a large frying pan over a high heat, and bring to the boil.

❷ Add the chicken, garlic and fish sauce to the frying pan and bring back to the boil. Lower the heat and simmer gently for 30 minutes, or until the chicken is tender.

❸ Remove the chicken from the mixture with a slotted spoon and set aside and keep warm.

❹ Stir the green curry paste into the frying pan, then add the aubergines, chillies and lime leaves, and simmer for 5 minutes.

❺ Return the chicken to the pan and bring to the boil. Adjust the seasoning to taste with salt and pepper, then stir in the coriander. Serve the curry with plain rice.

 extremely easy

 serves 4

 5 minutes

⏱ 55 minutes

COOK'S TIP

Baby aubergines, also
called 'Thai apple' or
'Thai pea' aubergines,
are traditionally used
in this curry. If you
cannot buy them in an
Asian food shop, the
mild, slender Japanese
aubergine would be
a good substitute,
chopped small.

Braised Chicken with Garlic & Spices

INGREDIENTS

4 garlic cloves, chopped
4 shallots, chopped
2 small red chillies,
  deseeded and
  chopped
1 lemon grass stalk,
  chopped finely
1 tbsp chopped fresh
  coriander
1 tsp shrimp paste
½ tsp ground cinnamon
1 tbsp tamarind paste
2 tbsp vegetable oil
8 small chicken
  drumsticks or thighs
300 ml/10 fl oz chicken
  stock
1 tbsp Thai fish sauce
1 tbsp smooth peanut
  butter
salt and pepper
4 tbsp chopped toasted
  peanuts

❶ Place the garlic, shallots, chillies, lemon grass, coriander and shrimp paste in a mortar and grind them with a pestle to an almost smooth paste. Add the cinnamon and tamarind paste.

❷ Heat the oil in a wok or a wide frying pan. Add the chicken drumsticks and fry them, turning often, until they are golden brown on all sides. Remove them from the wok and keep hot. Pour off any excess fat.

❸ Add the spice paste to the wok or pan, and stir over a medium heat until lightly browned. Stir in the stock, and return the chicken to the wok.

❹ Bring the mixture to the boil, then cover tightly, lower the heat, and simmer for 25–30 minutes, stirring occasionally, until the chicken is tender and cooked thoroughly. Stir in the fish sauce and peanut butter, and simmer gently for another 10 minutes.

❺ Adjust the seasoning with salt and pepper to taste and scatter the toasted peanuts over the chicken. Serve the dish hot, with colourful stir-fried vegetables and noodles.

 very easy

 serves 4

 10 minutes

 35 minutes

Wholemeal Spaghetti with Suprêmes of Chicken Nell Gwyn

INGREDIENTS

25 ml/1 fl oz rapeseed oil
3 tbsp olive oil
4 x 225 g/8 oz chicken suprêmes
150 ml/5 fl oz orange brandy
15 g/ ½ oz plain flour
150 ml/5 fl oz freshly squeezed orange juice
25 g/1 oz courgette, cut into matchsticks
25 g/1 oz red pepper, cut into matchsticks
25 g/1 oz leek, shredded
400 g/14 oz dried wholemeal spaghetti
3 large oranges, peeled and cut into segments
rind of 1 orange, cut into very fine strips
2 tbsp chopped fresh tarragon
⅔ cup fromage frais or ricotta cheese
salt and pepper
fresh tarragon leaves, to garnish

❶ Heat the rapeseed oil and 1 tablespoon of the olive oil in a frying pan. Add the chicken and fry quickly until golden brown. Add the orange brandy and cook for 3 minutes. Sprinkle the flour over the mixture and cook for 2 minutes.

❷ Lower the heat and add the orange juice, courgette, pepper and leek, and season. Simmer for 5 minutes, or until the sauce has thickened.

❸ Meanwhile, bring a pan of salted water to the boil. Add the spaghetti and 1 tablespoon of the olive oil, and cook for 10 minutes. Drain, transfer to a serving dish, and drizzle the remaining oil over the pasta.

❹ Add half the orange segments, half the orange rind, the tarragon and fromage frais or ricotta cheese to the sauce in the frying pan, and cook for 3 minutes.

❺ Place the chicken on top of the pasta, pour a little sauce over the top, and garnish with orange segments, rind and tarragon leaves. Serve immediately.

 very easy

 serves 4

 15 minutes

about 30 minutes

Chicken & Wild Mushroom Lasagne

butter, for greasing
14 sheets pre-cooked
  lasagne
850 ml/1½ pints
  béchamel sauce
85 g/3 oz grated
  Parmesan cheese

CHICKEN & WILD
MUSHROOM SAUCE
2 tbsp olive oil
2 garlic cloves, crushed
1 large onion, chopped
  finely
225 g/8 oz wild
  mushrooms, sliced
300 g/10½ oz minced
  chicken
85 g/3 oz chicken livers,
  chopped finely
115 g/4 oz Parma ham,
  diced
150 ml/ 5 fl oz Marsala
  wine
280 g/10 oz canned
  chopped tomatoes
1 tbsp chopped fresh
  basil leaves
2 tbsp tomato purée
salt and pepper

❶ Begin by making a chicken and wild mushroom sauce. Heat the olive oil in a large saucepan, add the garlic, onion and mushrooms, and fry, stirring frequently, for 6 minutes.

❷ Add the minced chicken, chicken livers and Parma ham, and continue frying over a low heat for 12 minutes, or until the meat has browned.

❸ Stir the Marsala wine, tomatoes, basil and tomato purée into the mixture in the pan, and cook for 4 minutes. Season to taste with salt and pepper, cover, and simmer for 30 minutes. Uncover the saucepan, stir, and simmer for another 15 minutes.

❹ Grease an ovenproof dish lightly with butter. Arrange sheets of lasagne over the base of the dish, spoon a layer of chicken and wild mushroom sauce over them, then spoon a layer of béchamel sauce over the top. Place another layer of lasagne on top, and repeat the layering twice, finishing with a layer of béchamel sauce. Sprinkle the grated cheese over the top layer, and bake the lasagne in a preheated oven at 190°C/375°F/Gas Mark 5 for 35 minutes, or until golden brown and bubbling. Serve immediately.

 easy

 serves 4

 20 minutes

 1¾ hours

Chicken with Green Olives & Pasta

INGREDIENTS

3 tbsp olive oil
25 g/1 oz butter
4 chicken breasts, part- boned
1 large onion, chopped finely
2 garlic cloves, crushed
2 red, yellow or green peppers, cored, seeded and cut into large pieces
250 g/9 oz button mushrooms, sliced or quartered
175 g/6 oz tomatoes, skinned and halved
150 ml/5 fl oz dry white wine
175 g/6 oz stoned green olives
50–90 ml/2–3¼ fl oz double cream
400 g/14 oz dried pasta
salt and pepper
chopped flat-leaved parsley, to garnish

❶ Heat 2 tablespoons of the oil and the butter in a frying pan. Add the chicken breasts and fry until they are golden brown all over. Remove the chicken from the pan.

❷ Add the onion and garlic to the pan and fry over a medium heat until they begin to soften. Add the peppers and mushrooms, and fry for 2–3 minutes. Add the tomatoes and season to taste. Transfer the vegetables to a casserole dish and arrange the chicken on top of them.

❸ Add the wine to the pan and bring it to the boil. Pour the wine over the chicken. Cover, and cook in a preheated oven at 180°C/350°F/Gas Mark 4 for 50 minutes.

❹ Add the olives to the casserole and mix them in. Pour in the cream, cover, and return to the oven for 10–20 minutes.

❺ Meanwhile, bring a large pan of lightly salted water to the boil. Add the pasta and the remaining oil and, cook until the pasta is tender but still firm to the bite. Drain the pasta well and transfer it to a serving dish.

❻ Arrange the chicken on top of the pasta, spoon the sauce over the top, garnish with the parsley, and serve immediately. Alternatively, place the pasta in a large serving bowl and serve it separately from the vegetables.

very easy

serves 4

10 minutes

1½ hours

Creamy Chicken & Potato Casserole

INGREDIENTS

2 tbsp vegetable oil
4 chicken portions,
　about 225 g/8 oz each
2 leeks, sliced
1 garlic clove, crushed
55 g/2 oz plain flour
900 ml/1½ pints chicken
　stock
300 ml/10 fl oz dry white
　wine
125 g/4½ oz baby
　carrots, halved
　lengthways
125 g/4½ oz baby
　sweetcorn, halved
　lengthways
450 g/1 lb small new
　potatoes
1 bouquet garni
150 ml/5 fl oz double
　cream
salt and pepper

❶ Heat the oil in a large frying pan. Fry the chicken portions for 10 minutes, turning until browned all over. Transfer the chicken to a casserole dish using a perforated spoon.

❷ Add the leek and garlic to the frying pan, and fry for 2–3 minutes, stirring. Stir in the flour and cook for another minute. Remove the frying pan from the heat, and stir in the stock and wine. Season well.

❸ Return the pan to the heat and bring the mixture slowly to the boil. Stir in the carrots, sweetcorn, potatoes and bouquet garni.

❹ Transfer the mixture to the casserole dish. Cover and cook in a preheated oven, 180°C/350°F/Gas Mark 4, for about 1 hour.

❺ Remove the casserole from the oven and stir in the cream. Return the casserole to the oven uncovered, and cook for another 15 minutes. Remove the bouquet garni and discard it. Taste and adjust the seasoning, if necessary, and serve the casserole with plain rice or fresh vegetables, such as broccoli.

 very easy

 serves 4

 10 minutes

 1 hour 40 minutes

Potato Crisp Pie

 easy

 serves 4

 15 minutes

 45 minutes

❶ Slice the potatoes and cook them in a saucepan of boiling water for 10 minutes. Drain and set aside.

❷ Meanwhile, melt the butter in a frying pan. Cut the chicken into strips and cook for 5 minutes, turning. Add the garlic and spring onions and cook for another 2 minutes.

❸ Stir in the flour and cook for 1 minute. Gradually add the wine and cream. Bring to the boil, stirring, reduce the heat until the sauce is simmering, then cook for 5 minutes.

❹ Meanwhile, blanch the broccoli in boiling water, drain, and refresh in cold water.

❺ Place half of the potatoes in the base of a pie dish, and top with half of the tomatoes and half of the broccoli.

❻ Spoon the chicken sauce on top and repeat the layers in the same order once more.

❼ Arrange the Gruyère cheese on top and spoon the yogurt over the top. Sprinkle with the oats and cook in a preheated oven, 200°C/400°F/Gas Mark 6, for 25 minutes, or until the top is golden brown. Serve the pie immediately.

VARIATIONS

Add chopped nuts, such as pine kernels, to the topping for extra crunch.

Chicken with a Creamy Courgette & Lime Stuffing

1 chicken, weighing
  2.25 kg/5 lb
oil for brushing
250 g/9 oz courgettes
25 g/1 oz butter
juice of 1 lime

STUFFING
85 g/3 oz courgettes
85 g/3 oz medium-fat
  soft cheese
finely grated rind of
  1 lime
2 tbsp fresh
  breadcrumbs
salt and pepper

 easy

 serves 4

 15 minutes

 1 hour,
50 minutes

VARIATIONS
For quicker cooking,
grate the courgettes
finely rather than cut
them into strips.

❶ To make the stuffing, trim the courgettes and grate them coarsely, and mix them with the cheese, lime rind, breadcrumbs, salt and pepper.

❷ Ease the skin away from the breast of the chicken.

❸ Push the stuffing under the skin with your fingers to cover the breast evenly.

❹ Place the chicken in a baking tin, brush it with oil, and roast it in a preheated oven, 190°C/375°F/Gas Mark 5, for 20 minutes per 500 g/1 lb 2 oz plus 20 minutes, or until the juices run clear when the thickest part of the chicken is pierced with a skewer.

❺ Meanwhile, trim the remaining courgettes and cut them into long, thin strips with a potato peeler or a sharp knife. Sauté the strips in the butter and lime juice until they are just tender. Place the cooked chicken on a serving plate and scatter the sautéed courgettes around it. Serve hot.

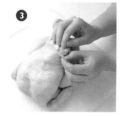